Abracadabra
VIOLA

Peter Davey

Contents

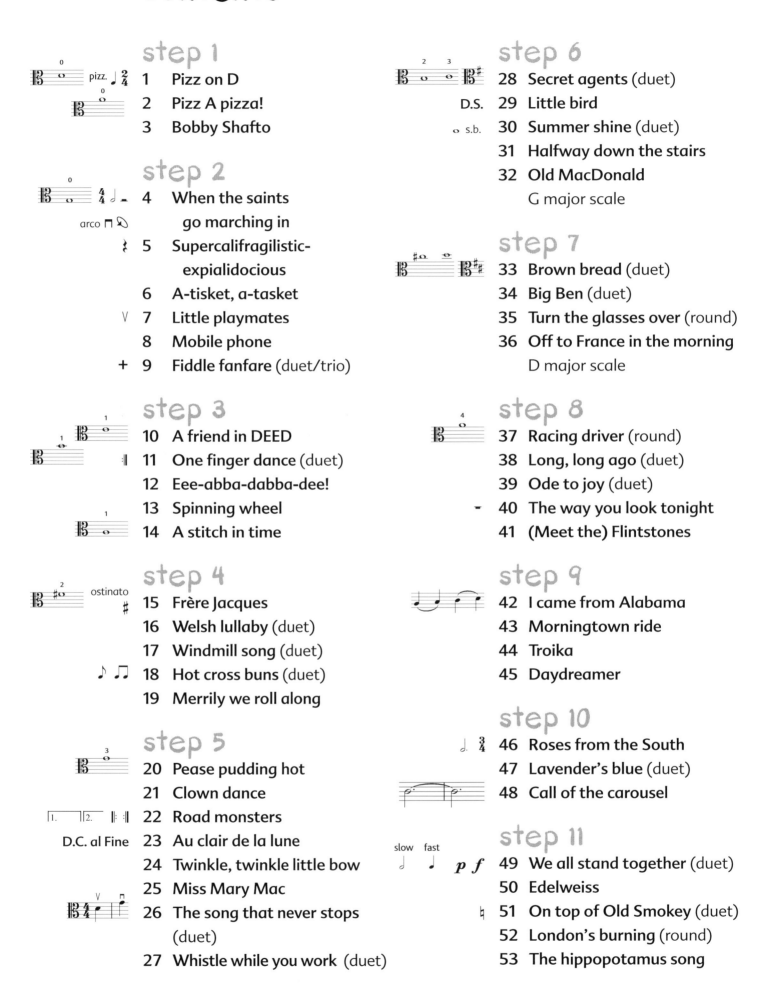

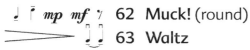

step 1

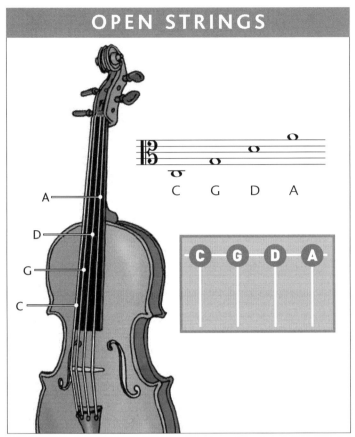

C   G   D   A

C   G   D   A

 Pluck your viola strings to play the tunes in step 1. This technique is called **pizzicato**, or **pizz**.

♩ **crotchet** – worth one beat.

$\frac{2}{4}$ **time signature** – this means there are two crotchet beats to the bar.

Play your part in *Pizz on D* twice.

1 Pizz on D   2-3

CH/VSP

You

pizz.

Piz - zi - ca - to,   squashed to - ma - to.

Your teacher

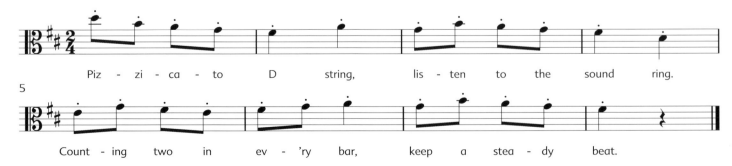

Piz - zi - ca - to   D   string,   lis - ten to the sound ring.

5

Count - ing two in ev - 'ry bar,   keep a stea - dy beat.

Play your part in *Pizz A pizza!* twice.

To make a longer piece, play *Pizz on D*, *Pizz A pizza!* and *Pizz on D* again, without pausing between the tunes.

2 Pizz A pizza! 4-5

CH/JS

You

pizz.

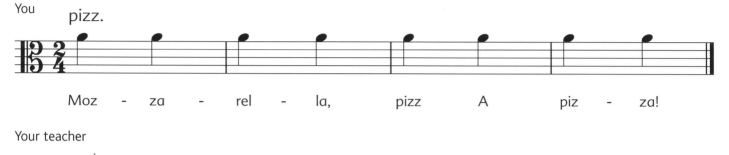

Moz – za – rel – la, pizz A piz – za!

Your teacher

pizz.

Chee – sy piz – za, Mar – ghe – ri – ta, That's my fav – 'rite tea – time treat.

3 Bobby Shafto 6-7

traditional

You

pizz.

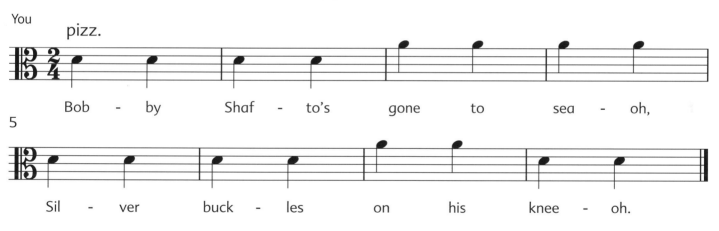

Bob – by Shaf – to's gone to sea – oh,

5

Sil – ver buck – les on his knee – oh.

Your teacher

pizz.

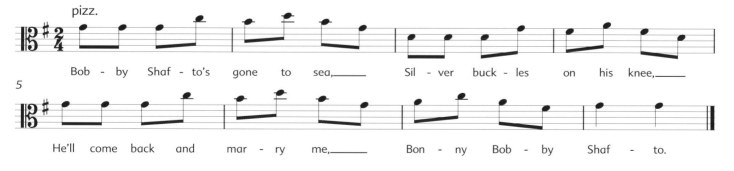

Bob – by Shaf – to's gone to sea,___ Sil – ver buck – les on his knee,___

5

He'll come back and mar – ry me,___ Bon – ny Bob – by Shaf – to.

 Play each of the tunes in step 1 twice through with your teacher.

1st time: you sing or say the words to your tune;
2nd time: ask your teacher to sing the words to their part.

step 2

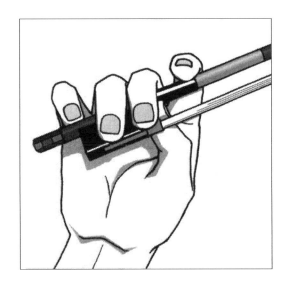

From heel
to point

 $\frac{4}{4}$ **time signature** – four crotchet beats to the bar.

♩ **minim** – worth two crotchet beats.

━ **minim rest** – it lasts for two crotchet beats of silence.

From now on, play all the tunes **arco** – with your bow – unless pizzicato is indicated.

⊓ marks a **down-bow**.

 tells you to lift your bow in a circular motion to prepare for the next down-bow.

4 When the saints go marching in 8-9
(pupil's part)

traditional spiritual

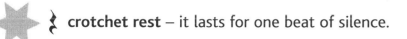
★ 𝄽 **crotchet rest** – it lasts for one beat of silence.

5 Supercalifragilisticexpialidocious (10-11)

Richard M Sherman and Robert B Sherman

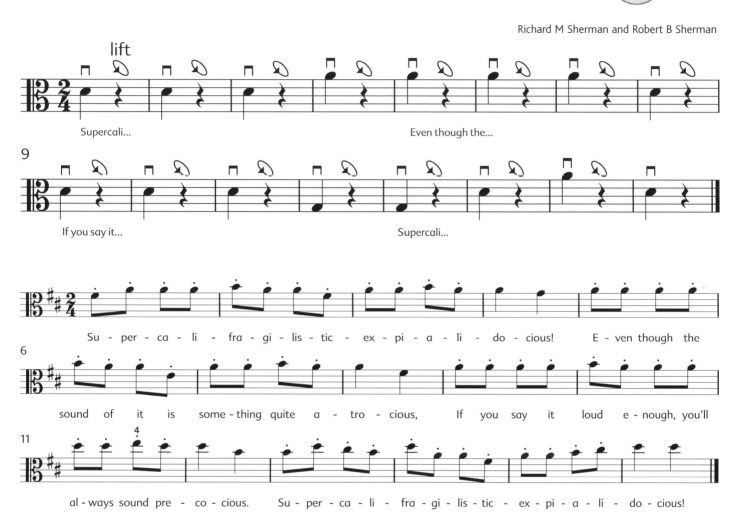

4 When the saints go marching in

(teacher's part)

6 A-tisket, a-tasket

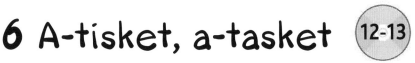

words CH, music traditional

1. A - tis - ket, a - tas - ket, There's some thing in my bas - ket, It
tas - ket, a - tis - ket, A choc - 'late or - ange bis - cuit, I'll

smells so sweet, it's good to eat, I'd bet you'd like to taste it. 2. A I don't want to waste it!
eat it now be - fore you can, 'Cos

 V marks an **up-bow**.

The bowing ⊓ V ⊓ tells you to play a **down-bow**, an **up-bow** and a **down-bow**, without lifting your bow off the string in between.

7 Little playmates

F X Chwatal

8 Mobile phone 16-17

words JS, music traditional

Count
1 2 +

My wife and I live all a - lone in a lit - tle log hut we call our own.

If we need to call the world, then we text it on our mo - bile phone!

⭐ **+** tells you to use your left hand to pluck the open string.

Play the crotchets ♩ in *Fiddle fanfare* with a half bow. Play the minims ♩ with a whole bow.

9 Fiddle fanfare (duet/trio) 18-19

CH

You

Your friend

pizz.
+

pizz.
+

pizz.
+

step 3

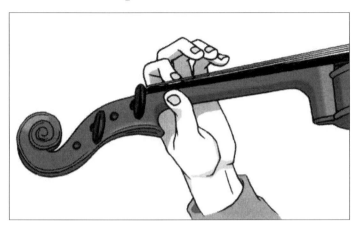

E

open —D—

1st finger (E)

1

E

 Play and sing this song with a friend.
It is like a conversation, in which you and your friend play question and answer phrases.

10 A friend in DEED 20-21

CH/JS

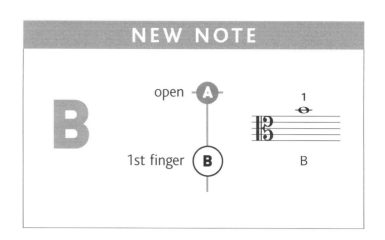

B   open A
1st finger B

1
B

:|| **repeat mark** – tells you to go back to the beginning and repeat the music.

In the second part of *One finger dance* the open strings D and A are played together – this is called **double stopping**.

11 One finger dance (duet) 22-23

PD

12 Eee-abba-dabba-dee! 24-25

CH

E   A   B B A,   D   A   B B A,

D   E E, Fred and me,   Eee - ab - ba - dab - ba - dee!

pizz.

13 Spinning wheel

Push   tread - le,   drive   spin - dle,   Round   goes   the   spin - ning   wheel.

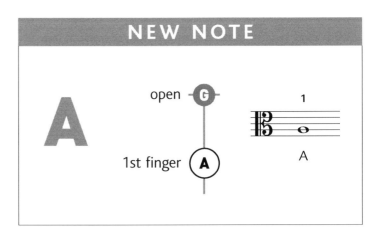

NEW NOTE

A

open — G

1st finger — A

A

14 A stitch in time

pizz. 1

Stitch in, stitch in,   stitch in time, A   stitch   in   time saves nine.

 Try playing **A stitch in time** while your teacher plays **Spinning wheel**.
Then swap over.

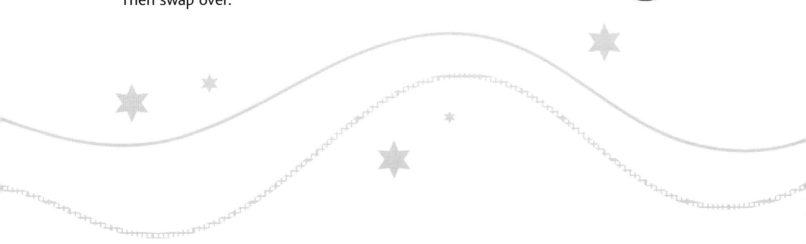

step 4

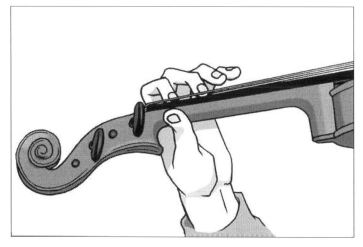

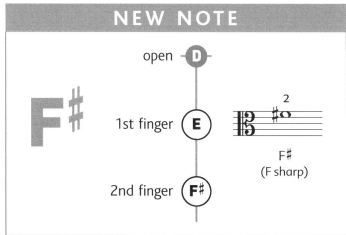

F♯

open — D
1st finger — E
2nd finger — F♯

F♯
(F sharp)

 ♯ is called a **sharp**. F♯ sounds a little higher than F.

In *Frère Jacques* you play a repeated one-bar phrase. A phrase repeated like this is called an **ostinato**.

15 Frère Jacques 32-33

traditional French

Ostinato 1

arco

Frè - re   Jac - ques,   Frè - re   Jac - ques,   Dor - mez   vous?   Dor - mez   vous?

Son - nez les ma - ti - nes!   Son - nez les ma - ti - nes!   Ding, dang, dong!   Ding, dang, dong!

 Play **Ostinato 2** eight times, while your teacher plays the tune. Then try the same with **Ostinato 3**.

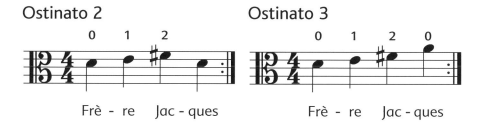

Ostinato 2

0 1 2

Frè - re   Jac - ques

Ostinato 3

0 1 2 0

Frè - re   Jac - ques

Play *Welsh lullaby* like this:

arco – for a baby dolphin

pizzicato – for a baby kangaroo

with your eyes shut – for a baby dormouse

16 Welsh lullaby (duet)

traditional Welsh

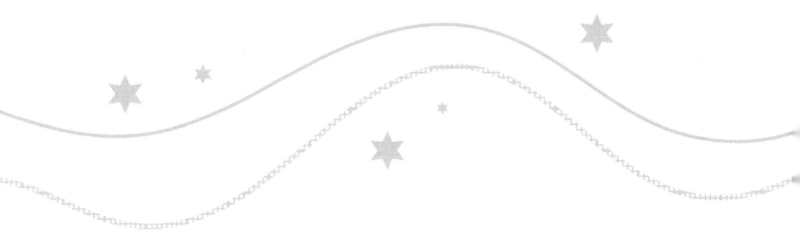

 ♯ The sharp sign affects all the notes of the same pitch in the rest of the bar.
For example, the fourth note in bar 1 of *Windmill song* is F♯ not F.

17 Windmill song (duet)

words CH, music PD

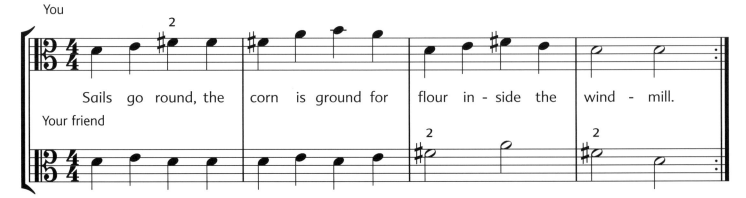

♪ **quaver** – worth half a crotchet beat.

Two quavers may be written like this:

The next two pieces begin on F♯, played with the 2nd finger. Make sure the F♯ is in tune before you start the piece. Climb up to it by playing D (open), then E (1st finger), then F♯ (2nd finger).

18 Hot cross buns (duet) 38-39

traditional

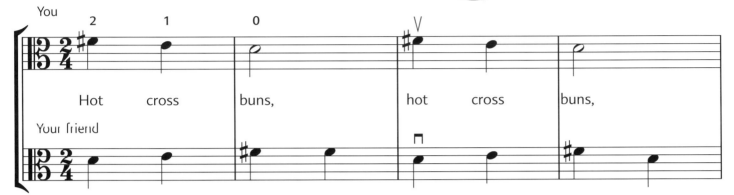

 Look at the last bar in no. 19. Do you remember the name of this technique? (Look at no. 11.)

19 Merrily we roll along 40-41

traditional

step 5

NEW NOTE

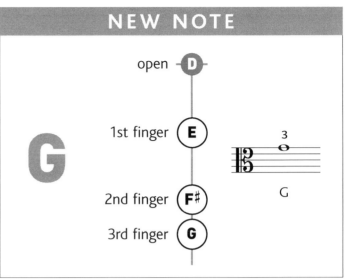

G

open — D
1st finger — E
2nd finger — F#
3rd finger — G

20 Pease pudding hot (42-43)

traditional

Pease   pud - ding   hot,   pease   pud - ding   cold.

Pease   pud - ding   in   the   pot   grow - ing   mould!

(arco)

pizz.

Ask your friend to play the ostinato accompaniment opposite.

21 Clown dance (44-45)

traditional French

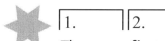

These are **first time** and **second time bars**. When you repeat the music, miss out the first time bar and go straight to the second time bar.

When there are two repeat marks, repeat the passage of music between them.

22 Road monsters 46-47

words CH/SR, music traditional Israeli

21 Ostinato accompaniment for *Clown dance*

D.C. al Fine tells you to repeat the music from the beginning up to **Fine**. **D.C.** is short for **Da Capo**, meaning from the beginning. **Fine** means end.

This piece begins on G, played with the 3rd finger. Make sure the G is in tune before you start the piece. Climb up to it by playing D (open), then E (1st finger), then F♯ (2nd finger), then G (3rd finger).

23 Au clair de la lune 48-49

traditional French

Play *Twinkle, twinkle little bow* twice – fast the first time and slowly the second time.

Hum the melody while your teacher plays the accompaniment. Watch your teacher's bowing action, especially in the middle section.

24 Twinkle, twinkle little bow 50-51

words JS, music traditional

(pupil's part)

Fine

Twin - kle, twin - kle   lit - tle   bow,   play   this   fast   then   play   it   slow.

D.C. al Fine

Draw   your   bow   a - cross   the   string,   care - ful   not   to   let   it   ping!

25 Miss Mary Mac (52-53)

traditional

Miss Ma - ry Mac, Mac, Mac, all dressed in

black, black, black, Her hair was long, long, long, all down her

back, back, back. Miss Ma - ry back.

24 Twinkle, twinkle little bow

(teacher's part)

Not all tunes begin on the first beat of the bar. Some start on the last beat of the bar, the **upbeat**. An **upbeat** is usually played with an up-bow.

When a piece begins on an **upbeat**, the final bar has one less beat than usual so that there are the correct number of beats in the piece.

Play the next song over and over without pausing in between. Find a way to end the piece. Then play it again, starting slowly and gradually getting faster each time.

26 The song that never stops (duet) CH

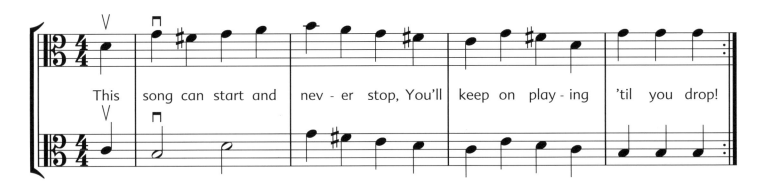

This | song can start and | nev - er stop, You'll | keep on play - ing | 'til you drop!

27 Whistle while you work (duet)

words Larry Morey,
music Frank Churchill

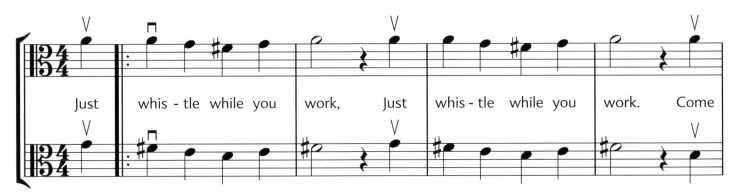

Just | whis - tle while you | work, Just | whis - tle while you | work. Come

5

on get smart, Tune | up and start to | whis - tle while you | work. Just | work.

step 6

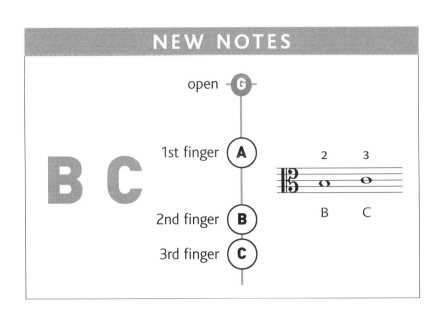

open — G

1st finger — A

B C

2nd finger — B

3rd finger — C

A **key signature** is written at the beginning of each line. This is the key signature for **G major**, in which all Fs are sharp (#).

28 Secret agents (duet) 58-59

words JS, music traditional

arco

Be a - ware and | take good care, Watch | out for sec - ret | a - gents.

pizz.

Codes to crack and | cars to chase, | Trails to track and | foes to face,

Be dis - creet in | all you do, 'Cos | a - gents might be | watch - ing you!

D.S. al Fine tells you to repeat the music from 𝄋 up to **Fine**. **D.S.** is short for **Dal Segno**, meaning 'from the sign'.

𝅝 **semibreve** – worth four crotchet beats.

s.b. is short for 'slow bow'. Use the whole of your bow to play any note marked **s.b.**

(⊓) tells you to play a down-bow on the repeat.

29 Little bird 60-61

traditional German

30 Summer shine (duet) 62-63

words CH, music PD

Ho - li - days are | on the way, | Clouds are gone, | days are long.

Sum - mer shine is | here to stay, | Lark will sing his | song.

Play *Summer shine* at the same speed as before, but play each note twice:

Use the middle of the bow to play the quavers and keep your bowing wrist relaxed.

etc.

31 Halfway down the stairs

words A A Milne,
music H Fraser Simson

Introduction

Half - way down the stairs is a stair where I sit: There

is - n't a - ny o - ther stair that's quite like it. I'm

not at the bot - tom and I'm not at the top: So

this is the stair where I al - ways stop.

Introduction

32 Old MacDonald

66-67

words adapted by SR, music traditional

Old Mac-Do-nald had a horse, ee - i - ee - i - oh! oh! With a

G, G here and a G, G there. Here a G, there a G, ev-'ry-where a G, G.

Old Mac - Do - nald had a horse, ee - i - ee - i - oh!

Here is the scale of G major.
The key signature is one sharp: F♯.

step 7

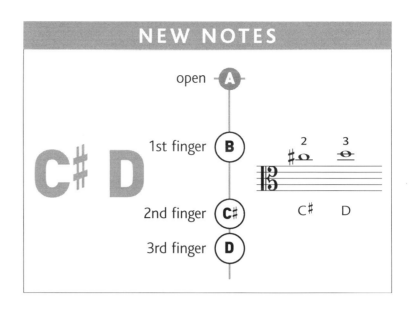

NEW NOTES

 This is the key signature for **D major**, in which all Fs and Cs are sharp (♯).

An instruction such as **Cheerfully** at the beginning of a piece tells you about the character of the music and how fast or slow it should be played.

These instructions are usually written in English or Italian. To find out what the Italian terms mean, look at the **glossary** at the back of the book.

Try playing the accompaniment to *Brown bread* pizzicato.

33 Brown bread (duet)

CH

34 Big Ben (duet)

traditional

Like clockwork

Big Ben all day long goes 'Ding, dong, ding, dong'. Small clocks

s.b.

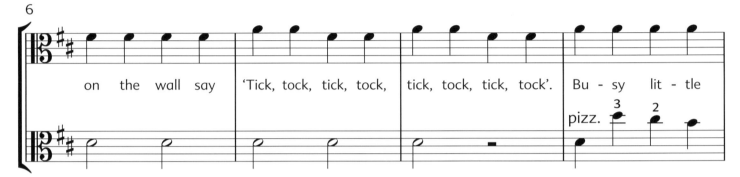

on the wall say 'Tick, tock, tick, tock, tick, tock, tick, tock'. Bu - sy lit - tle

pizz.

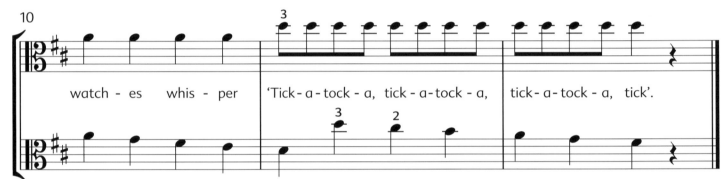

watch - es whis - per 'Tick-a-tock-a, tick-a-tock-a, tick-a-tock-a, tick'.

A **round** is a piece of music in which two or more people play or sing the same tune but start at different times. **Allegro** – fast and lively.

35 Turn the glasses over (round) 72-73

traditional

Allegro

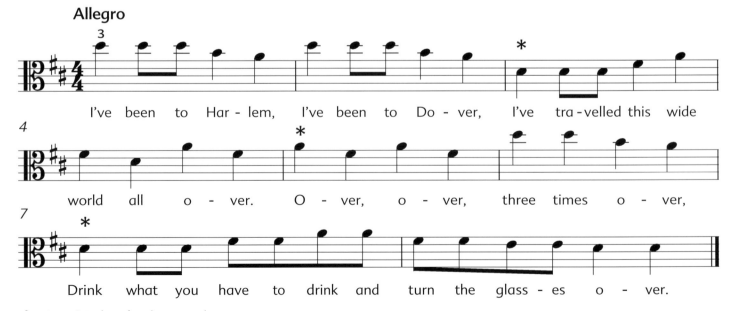

I've been to Har - lem, I've been to Do - ver, I've tra - velled this wide

world all o - ver. O - ver, o - ver, three times o - ver,

Drink what you have to drink and turn the glass - es o - ver.

✳ entry point when played as a round

36 Off to France in the morning

words CH, music PD

Brightly

Off to France, just for a day, Glad that it's not too far a-way.

Get-ting up at the crack of the dawn, When ev-'ry-one is yawn-ing.

Off on the train and I hope it won't rain, We'll sing out a song as we roll a-long.

I can't wait, let's ce-le-brate, 'Cos we're off to France in the morn-ing.

Here is the scale of D major. The key signature is two sharps: F♯ and C♯.

To practise reading in D major, play your teacher's part in no. 7 *Little playmates*.

FINGER PATTERN

	D	A
open	D	A
1st finger	E	B
2nd finger	F♯	C♯
3rd finger	G	D

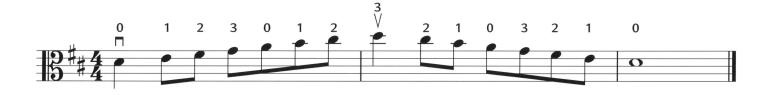

step 8

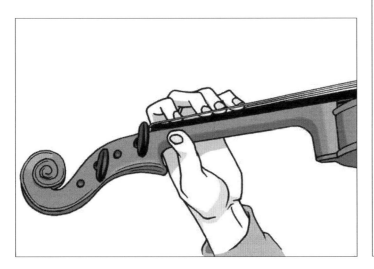

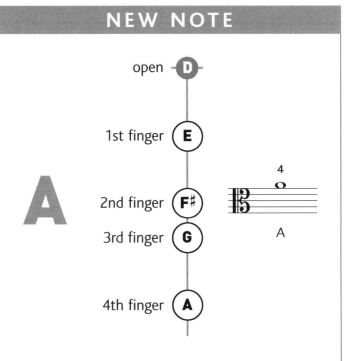

open — D —

1st finger — E

A   2nd finger — F♯

3rd finger — G

4th finger — A

4

A

 You can use either the open string or your **4th finger** to play the note A. The choice you make will depend on the notes before and after the note A.

In the following pieces the fingering is marked.

Do you recognise the tune of *Racing Driver*? (Look at no.15.)

Try playing this tune by ear, starting on the G string.

37 Racing driver (round)   76-77

words CH, music traditional French

Ra - cing dri - ver, ra - cing dri - ver, In your car, in your car,

Fill it up with pet - rol, fill it up with pet - rol, You'll go far, you'll go far.

✻ entry point when played as a round

Andante – at a leisurely pace.

38 Long, long ago (duet)

78-79

Thomas H Bayly

Tell me the tales that to | me were so dear, | Long, long a - go, | long, long a - go.

Sing me the songs I de- | light-ed to hear, | Long, long a - go, long a - | go.

39 Ode to joy (duet)

80-81

Ludwig van Beethoven

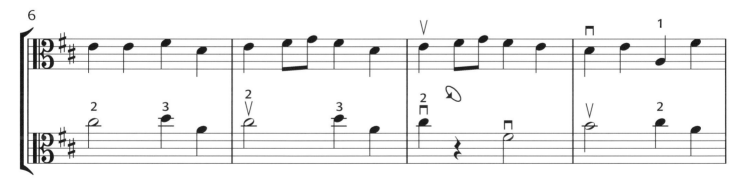

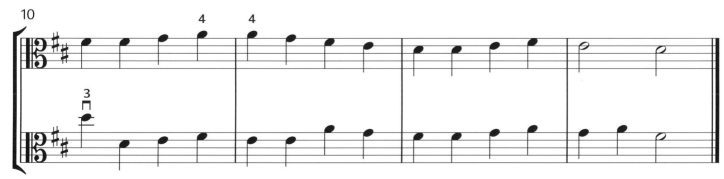

━ **semibreve rest** – lasts for four crotchet beats of silence.

Cantabile – in a singing style.

40 The way you look tonight

Jerome Kern

41 (Meet the) Flintstones

(teacher's part)

Aim to play this tune quickly, but practise slowly at first. Notice that there is a rest on the first beat of some bars.

41 (Meet the) Flintstones

Joseph Barbera, William Hanna and Hoyt Curtin

(pupil's part)

With energy

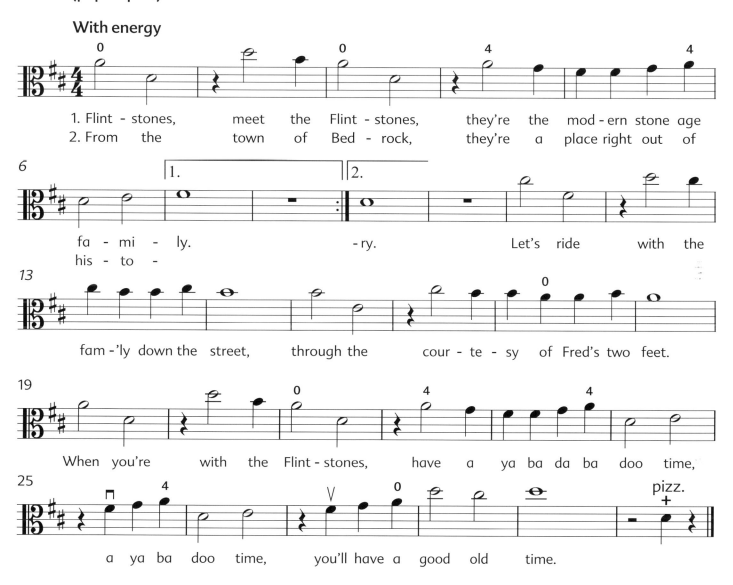

1. Flint - stones, meet the Flint - stones, they're the mod - ern stone age
2. From the town of Bed - rock, they're a place right out of

fa - mi - ly. - ry. Let's ride with the
his - to -

fam -'ly down the street, through the cour - te - sy of Fred's two feet.

When you're with the Flint - stones, have a ya ba da ba doo time,

a ya ba doo time, you'll have a good old time.

step 9

A **slur** joins two notes of different pitch and is played in one bow, which enables you to play smoothly.

The Italian term for playing smoothly is **legato**.

42 I came from Alabama

traditional North American, arr. CH

Accompaniment

Melody

43 Morningtown ride

88-89

Malvina Reynolds

44 Troika

90-91

Sergei Prokofiev

Light and lively

45 Daydreamer

92-93

CH

Legato

Think how day-dreams soothe, when all the ed-ges blur. To

make the mu-sic smooth, then join notes with a slur.

43 Morningtown ride (teacher's part continued)

step 10

$\frac{3}{4}$ This time signature shows that there are three crotchet beats in each bar.

𝅗𝅥. **dotted minim** – worth three crotchet beats.

A dot after a note makes it last longer by adding half the value of the original note.

2 + 1 = 3

𝅗𝅥 + ♩ = 𝅗𝅥.

46 Roses from the South 94-95

Johann Strauss II

Your friend

Your teacher

Dolce – sweetly.

47 Lavender's blue (duet) 2-3

traditional

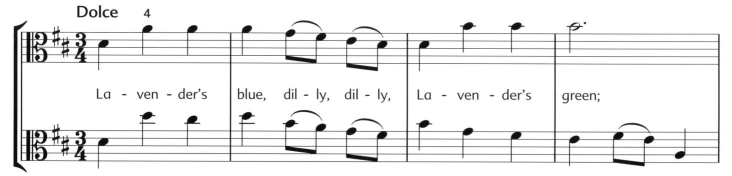

La - ven - der's blue, dil - ly, dil - ly, La - ven - der's green;

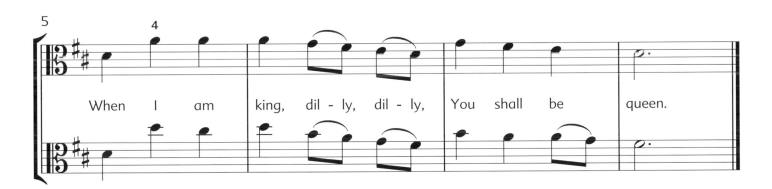

When I am king, dil - ly, dil - ly, You shall be queen.

 Two notes joined by a **tie** make one note which lasts the length of both notes.

Tied notes are played in one bow.

48 Call of the carousel

CH

step 11

 In this step you will practise a slow-fast bowing pattern in $\frac{3}{4}$

slow fast

Dynamics tell you how quietly or loudly to play.

p tells you to play quietly. It stands for **piano**, meaning 'quiet';

f tells you to play loudly. It stands for **forte**, meaning 'loud'.

49 We all stand together (duet)

Paul McCartney

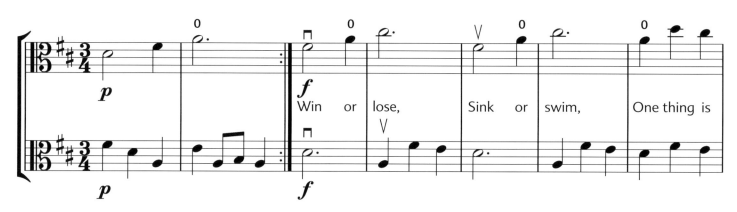

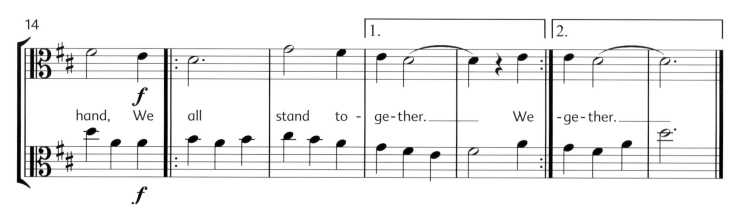

 **Espressivo** – expressively.

50 Edelweiss 8-9

words Oscar Hammerstein II, music Richard Rodgers

Espressivo

p E - del - weiss, E - del - weiss, Ev - 'ry morn - ing you

greet me. Small and white, Clean and bright,

You look hap - py to meet me. *f* Blos - som of snow, may you

bloom and grow, Bloom and grow for ev - er. *p* E - del -

- weiss, E - del - weiss, Bless my home - land for ev - er.

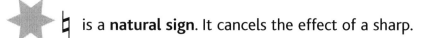 ♮ is a **natural sign**. It cancels the effect of a sharp.

51 On top of Old Smokey (duet)

 10-11

traditional North American

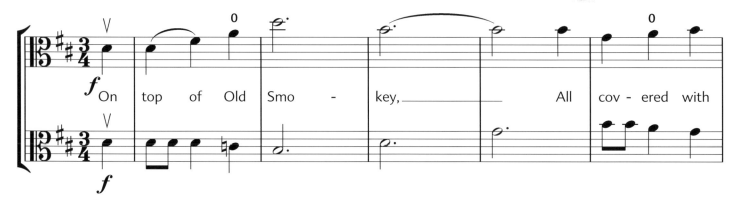

On top of Old Smo - key,_____ All cov - ered with

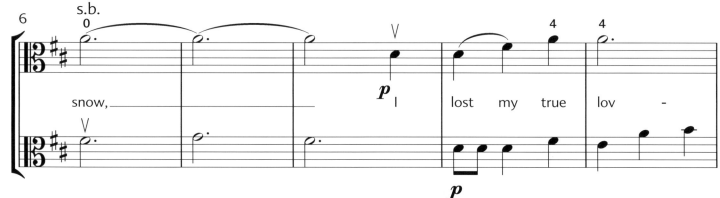

snow,_____ I lost my true lov -

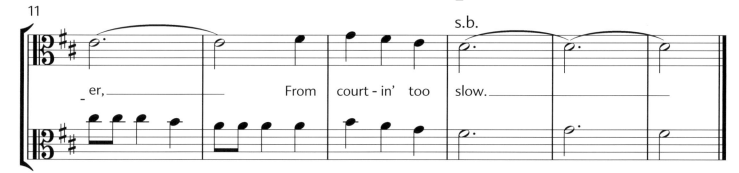

- er,_____ From court - in' too slow._____

 Con fuoco – with fire.

Play *London's burning* twice: 1st time *p*   2nd time *f*

52 London's burning (round)

 12-13

traditional

Con fuoco

Lon - don's burn - ing, Lon - don's burn - ing, Fetch the en - gines, fetch the

en - gines, Fire, fire! Fire, fire! Pour on wa - ter, pour on wa - ter.

✳ entry point when played as a round

53 The hippopotamus song

words Michael Flanders,
music Donald Swann

Waltz

Mud, mud, glo - ri - ous mud! No - thing quite like it for

cool - ing the blood. (So fol - low me, follow,____ down to the hollow,) And

there let us wal - low in glo - ri - ous mud.

(So fol - low me,

fol low,_ down to the hol low,)

step 12

★ ♩. **dotted crotchet** – worth one and a half crotchet beats:

$$1 + \tfrac{1}{2} = 1\tfrac{1}{2}$$

♩ + ♪ = ♩.

These two rhythms look different, but sound the same:

1   2 + 3
Lon - don Bridge

Lon - don Bridge

f.b. – fast bow.

54 London Bridge (duet) 16-17

traditional

 ★ **Leggiero** – lightly.

55 Tea for two (pupil's part) 18-19

words Irving Caesar,
music Vincent Youmans, arr. CH

To practise dotted rhythms, play your teacher's part in

no. 42 *I came from Alabama*
no. 4 *When the saints go marching in*
no. 6 *A-tisket, a-tasket*

56 Stand by me

Ben E King, Jerry Leiber and Mike Stoller, arr. CH

Rhythmically

When the night has come ____ and the land is dark, And the moon ____ is the

on - ly ____ light we'll see. No I won't be a - fraid, No I ____ won't be a -

-fraid, Just as long ____ as you stand, ____ stand by me. So dar - ling, dar - ling stand ____ by

me, Oh, ____ stand ____ by me, Oh, stand, ____ stand by ____ me, stand by ____ me.

55 Tea for two (teacher's part)

step 13

Learn this zig-zag technique, which uses the whole bow.

shows a ⊓ V ⊓ pattern

shows a V ⊓ V pattern

57 Skye boat song (duet) 22-23

traditional Scottish

Maestoso – majestically.

In *Jupiter*, use your 4th finger to play the note D on the G string when marked.

58 Jupiter (pupil's part) 24-25

Gustav Holst

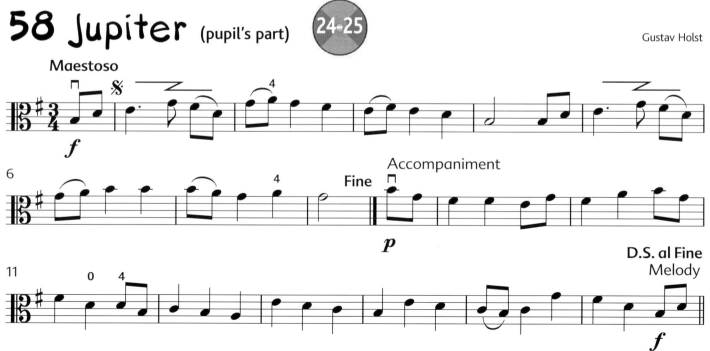

A **semibreve rest** can also be used to indicate a whole bar's rest in any time signature.

crescendo – tells you to get gradually louder.

59 Feed the birds

Richard M Sherman and Robert B Sherman

58 Jupiter (teacher's part)

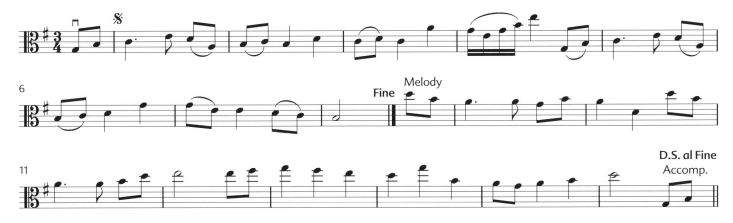

step 14

⭐ ♩ ♪ **staccato** – the dot tells you to make the note short and detached.

cresc. indicates a long crescendo. It tells you to get gradually louder until you reach the next dynamic mark.

Con spirito – with spirit.

Start *Kalinka* slowly and get gradually faster.

60 Kalinka 28-29

traditional Russian

To practise staccato notes, play your teacher's part in

no. 1 *Pizz on D*
no. 5 *Supercalifragilisticexpialidocious*

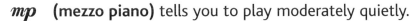

mp **(mezzo piano)** tells you to play moderately quietly.

mf **(mezzo forte)** tells you to play moderately loudly.

♩ ̄ A **tenuto** line tells you to hold the note for its full length.

⁊ **quaver rest** – lasts for half a crotchet beat of silence.

62 Muck! (round)

traditional

✱ entry point when played as a round

These are **non-legato ties**. They tell you to play both notes in the same bow, but to make them slightly detached by stopping the bow for a moment in mid-stroke. This technique is sometimes called **hooked bowing**.

diminuendo – tells you to get gradually quieter.

63 Waltz

Franz Lehar

Moderato – at a moderate speed.

64 Puff the magic dragon (duet)

Peter Yarrow and Leonard Upton

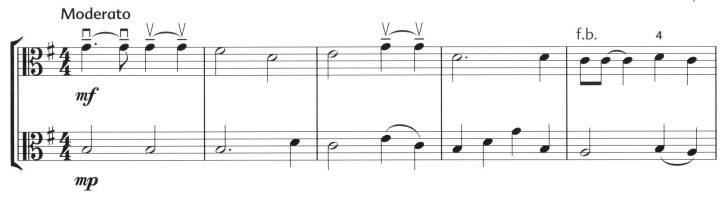

65 Dumplins

traditional Caribbean

'Ja - ney,   you see no-bo-dy   pass   here?'   'No   me   friend.'   friend.'   'Well

one of   me dump-lins   gone.' 'Don't tell___   me   so!'   'One of   me dump-lins   gone!'

step 15

 time signature – means there are six quaver beats to the bar.

Count six quavers:

or two dotted crotchets:

1 2

Try playing these rhythms on any open string:

66 Row, row, row your boat (round)

traditional

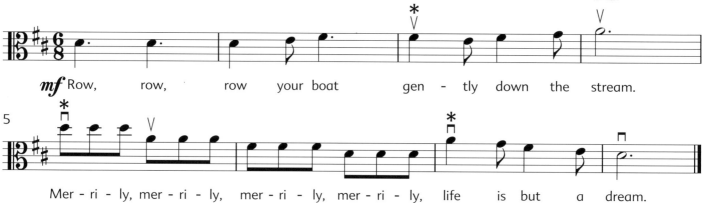

mf Row, row, row your boat gen - tly down the stream.

Mer - ri - ly, mer - ri - ly, mer - ri - ly, mer - ri - ly, life is but a dream.

✳ entry point when played as a round

67 Pop! goes the weasel

traditional

f Half a pound of tup - pen - ny rice, Half a pound of trea - cle,

That's the way the mon - ey goes, Pop! goes the wea - sel.

Ostinato accompaniment (play four times)

mf

Compose your own ostinato accompaniment to go with *Row, row, row your boat* or *Pop! goes the weasel*.

Play the open strings D and A and use any of the $\frac{6}{8}$ rhythms opposite.

68 Dance of the cuckoos (duet)

Marvin Hatley

69 The shepherdess (round)

traditional French

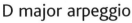 entry point when played as a round

D major arpeggio

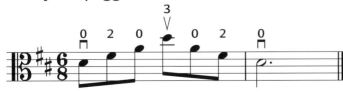

G major arpeggio

70 We're off to see the Wizard

words E Y Harburg, music Harold Arlen

Con spirito

mf We're off to see the Wiz-ard, the won-der-ful Wiz-ard of Oz. We

hear he is a whiz of a Wiz if ev-er a Wiz there was. *mp* If

ev-er, oh ev-er a Wiz there was, the Wiz-ard of Oz is one be-cause, be-

-cause, be-cause, be-cause, be-cause, be-cause, *f* Be-

-cause of the won-der-ful things he does. *mf* We're

off to see the Wiz-ard, the won-der-ful Wiz-ard of Oz.

step 16

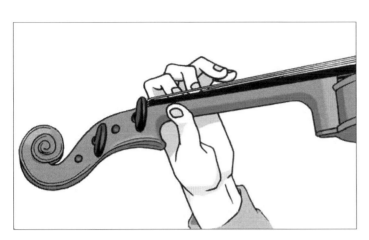

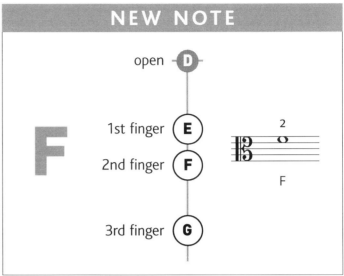
 F is halfway between E and F♯ – a semitone higher than E and a semitone lower than F♯.

Misterioso – mysteriously.

Try playing *Egyptian snake dance* pizzicato. Then play it arco, but make each note staccato (leaving out the slurs and ties).

71 Egyptian snake dance

traditional

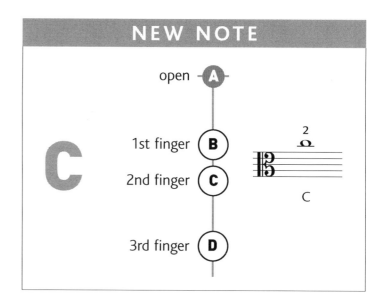

open — A

1st finger — B

2nd finger — C

3rd finger — D

C

72 Shalom (round) 52-53

traditional Israeli

Warmly

mp

Sha - lom, cha - ve - rim, sha - lom, cha - ve - rim, sha - lom, sha - lom. Le -

mp

-hi - tra - ot, le - hi - tra - ot, sha - lom, sha - lom.

✳ entry point when played as a round

73 Summer is icumen in (round) 54-55

traditional

Brightly

mf

mp

f

mf

✳ entry point when played as a round

74 Part of your world (duet)

words Howard Ashman,
music Alan Menken

step 17

♪ **semiquaver** – worth a quarter of a crotchet beat.

Semiquavers can be grouped like this: ♫ ♬

Look carefully at the key signature before you start each piece, so that you can decide where to place your second finger.

Look at the accompaniment for ***What shall we do with the drunken sailor?***
Check the key signature. What do you notice?

75 What shall we do with the drunken sailor? (duet)

traditional

  To practise semiquavers, play your teacher's part in no. 8 ***Mobile phone***.

76 Winter wonderland

words Richard Smith, music Felix Bernard

Sleigh bells ring, are you list - 'nin'! In the lane snow is

glist - 'nin', A beau - ti - ful sight, __ We're hap - py to - night, __

Walk - in' in a win - ter won - der - land! Sleigh bells -land!

77 EastEnders

Leslie Osborne and Simon May

step 18

⭐ All the tunes in this step use a mixture of both positions of the 2nd finger.

⌒ **pause** – tells you to hold a note for longer than its written value.

78 Happy birthday (duet)

Patty S Hill and Mildred Hill

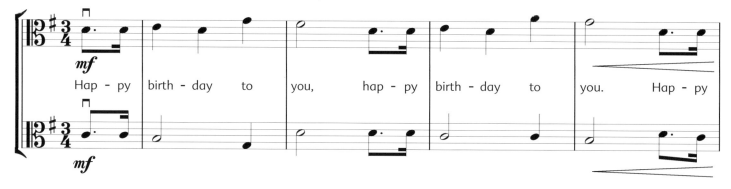

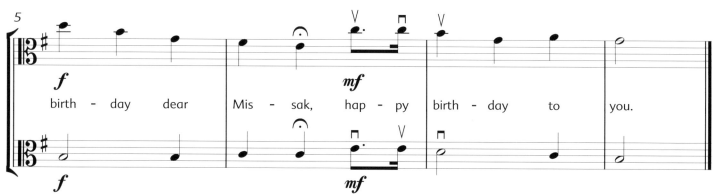

79 Heigh-ho

words Larry Morey, music Frank Churchill

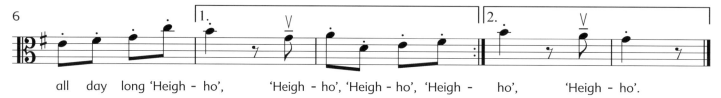

The next three tunes use both positions of the 2nd finger on the D string: F♯ and F.

Try playing *The Addams family* pizzicato to make it sound even spookier. Then ask your teacher to play the tune, while you do the finger clicks.

80 The Addams family (duet)

Vic Mizzy

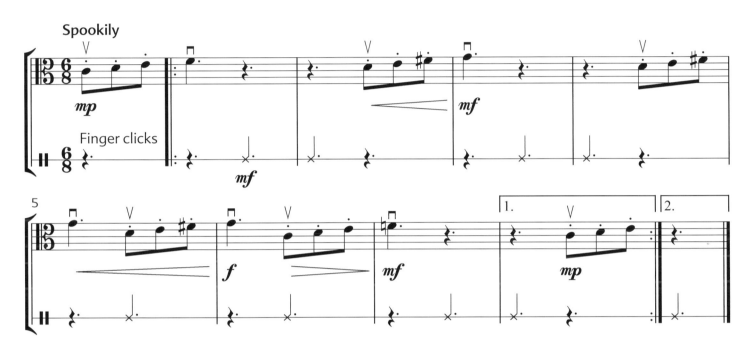

81 The mocking bird

traditional Caribbean

82 Chim chim cher-ee

Richard M Sherman and Robert B Sherman

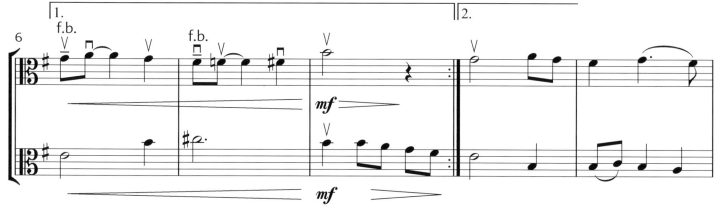

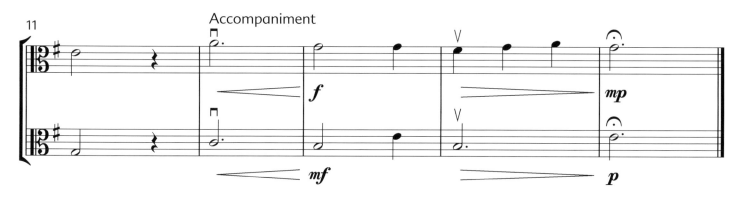

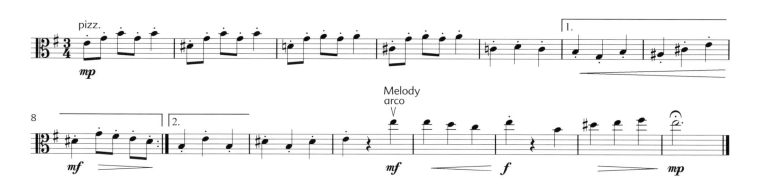

 To practise both positions of the 2nd finger, play your teacher's part in

no. 22 *Road monsters*

no. 3 *Bobby Shafto*

NEW NOTES

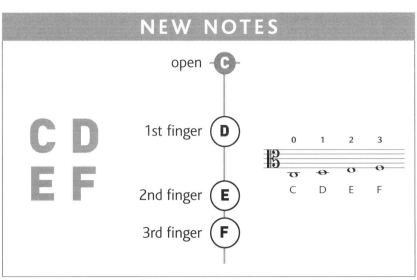

open — C

C D E F

1st finger — D

2nd finger — E

3rd finger — F

83 Ragamuffin's rag 74·75

CH

C major

scale (two octaves)

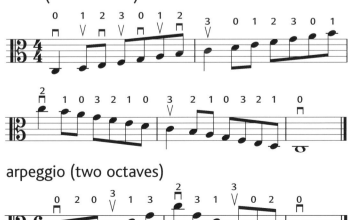

The finger pattern of the first octave is the same as that of D major, starting on the C string.

FINGER PATTERN

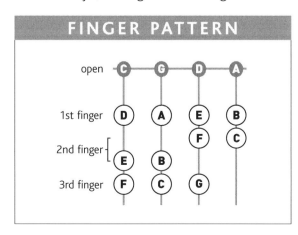

open — C — G — D — A

1st finger — D — A — E — B

2nd finger — E — B — F / C

3rd finger — F — C — G

arpeggio (two octaves)

84 Who will buy?

Lionel Bart

Melody

f

Who will buy this won-der-ful morn - ing? Such a sky you nev-er did see!___

Who will tie it up with a rib - bon, And put it in a box for me?

⭐ Playing this accompaniment will give you practise on the C string.

Pupil's accompaniment

f

p

Teacher's accompaniment

mf

p

85 Beauty and the Beast (duet)

words Howard Ashman, music Alan Menken

Andante

Tale as old as time, true as it can be.

Bare - ly e - ven friends, then some - bo - dy bends un - ex - pec - ted - ly.

Just a lit - tle change. Small, to say the least. Both a lit - tle

scared, nei - ther one pre - pared. Beau - ty and the Beast.

step 20

⭐ *Barcarolle* contains three-note slurs.
Play each slurred group of notes in one bow.

86 Barcarolle (duet)

Jacques Offenbach

⭐ **rall.** tells you to get gradually slower. It is short for **rallentando**.
Nocturne contains four-note slurs. Play all four notes in one bow.

87 Nocturne

Aleksander Borodin

Acknowledgements

The author and publisher would like to thank the following for their help in the preparation of this book: Jeremy Birchall, Patricia Birchall, Jennifer Boston, Adrian Bradbury, Emily Brayshaw, Chris Bryant, Helen Crayford, Janet Crew, Michelle Daley, Louise Dearsley, Tanya Demidova, Philip Dukes, Heather Fleck, David W Giles, Emily Haward, Jocelyn Lucus, Andrew Lynwood, Grace Lynwood, Barry Newland, Malcolm Pallant, Maja Passchier, Aoife Patarot-Hinds, Roland Roberts, Sheena Roberts, Valérie Saint-Pierre, Elaine Scott, Michelle Simpson, Holly Stirling, Dominic Viall, Matthew Watson and Allison Whitehead. Very special thanks go to Carla Moss.

We are grateful to the following copyright owners who have kindly granted permission for the reprinting of these items:

Beauty and the Beast (from Beauty and the Beast) Words by Howard Ashman, Music by Alan Menken, © 1991 Wonderland Music Company Inc and Walt Disney Music Co Ltd, USA. Warner/Chappell Artemis Music Ltd, London W6 8BS. Reproduced by permission of Faber Music Ltd. All Rights Reserved;

Chim chim cher-ee (From Mary Poppins) Words and Music by Richard M Sherman and Robert B Sherman © 1963 Wonderland Music Company Inc, Warner/Chappell Artemis Music Ltd, London W6 8BS. Reproduced by permission of Faber Music Ltd. All Rights Reserved;

Dance of the cuckoos (Ku-ku) By T Marvin Hatley © 1930, 1932 Hatley Music Company, USA. Robert Kingston Music Limited, 8/9 Frith Street, London W1. Used by permission of Music Sales Ltd. All Rights Reserved. International Copyright Secured;

Eastenders by Leslie Osborne & Simon May © 1985 ATV Music. Sony/ATV Music Publishing (UK) Limited, 10 Great Marlborough Street, London W1. Used by permission of Music Sales Ltd. All Rights Reserved. International Copyright Secured;

Edelweiss from the Sound of Music. Words by Oscar Hammerstein II, music by Richard Rodgers © 1959 by Richard Rodgers and Oscar Hammerstein II. Copyright renewed. This arrangement © 2002 by Williamson Music. Williamson Music owner of publication and allied rights throughout the world. International Copyright Secured. All Rights Reserved;

Feed the birds (from Mary Poppins) Music and Words by Richard M Sherman and Robert B Sherman © 1964 Wonderland Music Company Inc, Warner/Chappell Artemis Music Ltd, London W6 8BS. Reproduced by permission of Faber Music Ltd. All Rights Reserved;

Halfway down the stairs Text by A.A. Milne and Music by H. Fraser Simson. Copyright under the Berne Convention;

Happy birthday to you Words and Music by Patty S Hill and Mildred Hill © 1935 (renewed 1962) Summy Birchard Inc. Keith Prowse Music Publishing Co Ltd. Reproduced by International Music Publications (a trading name of Faber Music Ltd). All Rights Reserved;

Heigh ho Words by Larry Morey. Music by Frank Churchill © copyright 1938 by Bourne Co. Copyright Renewed. This arrangement © copyright 2002 by Bourne Co. All Rights Reserved. International Copyright Secured. Printed with permission from Bourne Music Ltd;

Lieutenant Kijé (Troika), op. 60 by Prokofieff. Copyright © 1936 by Hawkes & Son (London) Ltd. Reproduced by permission of Boosey & Hawkes Music Publishers Ltd;

(Meet) The Flintstones Words and Music by Joseph Barbera, William Hanna and Hoyt Curtin © 1960 Warner/Tamerlane Publishing Corp, USA. Warner/Chappell North America Ltd, Londond W6 8BS. Reproduced by permission of Faber Music Ltd. All Rights Reserved;

Morningtown ride © 1959 by Amadeo Brio Music Inc. Administered by MCS Music Ltd, 32 Lexington Street, London W1F OLQ;

Off to France in the morning, One finger dance, Spinning wheel, Summer shine and **Windmill song** © 1985 Peter Davey;

Part of your world (from The Little Mermaid) Music by Alan Menken, Words by Howard Ashman © 1988 Walt Disney Music (USA) Co Ltd and Wonderland Music Company Inc, USA. Warner/Chappell Artemis Music Ltd, London W6 8BS. Reproduced by permission of Faber Music Ltd. All Rights Reserved;

Puff the magic dragon Words and Music by Leonard Lipton and Peter Yarrow. Copyright © 1963 Pepamar Music Corp and Honalee Melodies, USA (70%) Warner/Chappell North America Ltd. 30% Cherry Lane Music Publishing Inc. Reproduced by permission of Faber Music Ltd. All Rights Reserved;

Stand by me Words and music by Ben E King, Jerry Leiber and Mike Stoller © 1961 (renewed) Jerry Leiber Music, Mike Stoller Music and Trio Music Company INC. This arrangement © 2002 Jerry Leiber Music, Mike Stoller Music and Trio Music Company INC. All Rights Reserved;

Supercalifragilisticexpialidocious (From Mary Poppins) Words and Music by Richard M Sherman and Robert B Sherman © 1964 Wonderland Music Company Inc, Warner/Chappell Artemis Music Ltd, London W6 8BS. Reproduced by permission of Faber Music Ltd. All Rights Reserved;

Tea for two Words by Irving Caesar, music by Vincent Youmans © 1924 Harms Inc, USA (50%) Chappell Music Ltd and (50%) Warner/Chappell Music Ltd, London W6 8BS. Reproduced by permission of Faber Music Ltd. All Rights Reserved;

The Addams family Words and Music by Vic Mizzy © 1963 Unison Music Publishing Co Ltd. EMI Music Publishing Ltd. Reproduced by permission of International Music Publications Ltd (a trading name of Faber Music Ltd). All Rights Reserved;

The hippopotamus song Words by Michael Flanders, Music by Donald Swann © 1952 Chappell Music Ltd, London W6 8BS. Reproduced by permission of Faber Music Ltd. All Rights Reserved;

The way you look tonight Words by Dorothy Fields, Music by Jerome Kern © 1936 T B Harms Company and Aldi Music, USA (50%) Shapiro Bernstein & Co Limited, New York NY 10022-5718, USA. Reproduced by permission of Faber Music Ltd. All Rights Reserved;

Waltz from The Merry Widow Music by Franz Lehar. © 1928 Ludwig KG Doblinger Musik-Verlag. Chappell Music Ltd. Reproduced by permission of Faber Music Ltd. All Rights Reserved;

We All Stand Together by Paul McCartney © 1984 (Renewed) MPL Communications Ltd. All Rights Reserved, Used By Permission;

We're off to see the wizard Words by E Y Harburg, music by Harold Arlen © 1939 EMI Catalogue Partnership, EMI Feist Catalog Inc and EMI United Partnership Ltd, USA. Worldwide print rights controlled by Warner Bros. Reproduced by permission of Faber Music Ltd. All Rights Reserved;

Whistle while you work Words by Larry Morey. Music by Frank Churchill. © copyright 1937 by Bourne Co. All Rights Reserved. International Copyright Secured. Printed with permission from Bourne Music Ltd;

Who will buy? © 1960 Lakeview Music Publishing Co Ltd. Suite 2.07, Plaza 535 Kings Road, London SW10 0SZ. International Copyright Secured. All Rights Reserved. Used by permission;

Winter wonderland Words by Dick Smith, Music by Felix Bernard © 1934 Francis Day & Hunter Ltd (For Europe excl. France, Belgium, Monaco, Italy, Spain, Portugal, Holland & French-speaking part of Switzerland) and Warner/Chappell North America ltd (For France, Belgium, Monaco, Italy, Spain, Portugal, Holland & French-speaking part of Switzerland). Reproduced by permission of International Music Publications Ltd (a trading name of Faber Music Ltd) and Faber Music Limited. All Rights Reserved.

All other original pieces and arrangements are copyright HarperCollins*Publishers* Ltd. Every effort has been made to trace and acknowledge copyright owners. If any right has been omitted, the publishers offer their apologies and will rectify this in subsequent editions following notification.

Recording

Viola – Philip Dukes
Piano – Helen Crayford
Engineered by Matthew Moore and Andrew Lynwood
All other arrangements by Barry Gibson (5, 22, 43, 60, 84)
and David Moses (10, 31, 58, 70, 88)

All rights reserved. Copying, public performance and broadcasting – in whole or in part – of the recording are prohibited by law.

INDEX

GLOSSARY

⊓	down-bow	$\boldsymbol{p}$	(piano) quiet
V	up-bow	$\boldsymbol{f}$	(forte) loud
↻	lift bow in circular motion	$\boldsymbol{mp}$	(mezzo piano) moderately quiet
+	left-hand pizzicato	$\boldsymbol{mf}$	(mezzo forte) moderately loud
D.C. al Fine	repeat from the beginning (Da Capo) up to Fine (the end)		
D.S. al Fine	repeat from 𝄋 (the sign) up to Fine (the end)		
s.b.	slow bow		
f.b.	fast bow	allegro	– fast and lively
⊓ V ⊓	zig-zag bowing pattern	andante	– at a leisurely pace
V ⊓ V	zig-zag bowing pattern	cantabile	– in a singing style
	crescendo – get gradually louder	con fuoco	– with fire
	diminuendo – get gradually quieter	con spirito	– with spirit
		dolce	– sweetly
⌢	pause	espressivo	– expressively
arco	with bow	legato	– smoothly
ostinato	a repeated musical phrase	leggiero	– lightly
pizzicato (pizz.)	plucked	maestoso	– majestically
rallentando (rall.)	get gradually slower	misterioso	– mysteriously
staccato	short and detached	moderato	– at a moderate speed
tenuto	with a light accent, lasting full length	tempo di valse	– like a waltz